Original title:
Melon and Mint

Copyright © 2025 Creative Arts Management OÜ
All rights reserved.

Author: Harrison Blake
ISBN HARDBACK: 978-1-80586-431-8
ISBN PAPERBACK: 978-1-80586-903-0

A Taste of the Dream

A fruit so bright, a flavor blast,
Beneath the sun, we find the past.
With every slice, a giggle too,
It's juicy joy, just me and you.

A twist of green, a dance in bowls,
Like happy frogs, it jives and rolls.
Sticky fingers, laughter spills,
Chasing sweetness gives us thrills.

Sipping smoothies, topsy-turvy,
A splash of cheer, oh so flirty.
We blend and whirl, the craziness grows,
In every sip, the laughter flows.

So gather round, our fruity cheer,
The taste of fun is finally here.
With bites of joy, we celebrate,
A fruity feast, oh what a fate!

Essence of Summer's Touch

In sunlit days, we catch the zest,
A burst of glee, we feel the best.
Laughter floats on warm, soft air,
With every munch, we shed our care.

Zippy slices on our plates,
Crown the day, like silly mates.
Mix and mingle, taste the spree,
A festival of taste, just you and me.

Round and round, the juicy game,
Each burst of flavor, never the same.
A sticky smile, a splat, a squish,
Each little nibble, a funny wish.

So let's embrace the silly fun,
With every bite, we weigh a ton!
While giggles echo through the noon,
Our favorite dish, a funny tune!

Effervescent Impressions

Bubbles pop in summer's glow,
Sweetness dancing, what a show.
Sips so sharp, a twist of zest,
Making taste buds feel the best.

Laughter flows like fizzy cheer,
Sipping sunshine, joy is near.
Swirling flavors, bright and bold,
Tales of summer, freshly told.

Springtime Rhapsody

Greenery bursts with cheerful flair,
Nature's giggle in the air.
Juicy bursts like playful jives,
Happiness in every slice.

Bouncy vibes in every bite,
Taste buds sing with pure delight.
Silly sounds of bliss surround,
In this garden, joys abound.

Nature's Green Elixir

A splash of laughter, a hint of fun,
Refreshing zest, a race to run.
Chasing echoes of sweet delight,
Sipping breezes, day turns night.

Green delight in every glass,
Whispered tales as good times pass.
Breezy giggles, joy we share,
In this magic, no compare.

Crystal Clear Essence

Clear and bright, a fizzy dance,
Lifted spirits, take a chance.
Sips of laughter, oh so sweet,
Every drop's a happy treat.

Joyful bubbles, rise and play,
Tasting sunshine, bright as day.
With each pour, the fun expands,
Life's a party, drink in hands.

A Dance of Leaves and Sunlight

In the garden, colors bright,
A twist of green, a bite of light.
The fruit with stripes, a treat in hand,
Giggles echo across the land.

Sipping shades from glasses clear,
Laughter bubbles, joy is near.
Each juicy bite brings sunny cheer,
As nature laughs, we draw it near.

Serene Pools of Flavor

A splash of sweetness flows so bright,
Chilled delight on a warm, warm night.
Round and plump, the joy we seek,
A whisper soft, no need to speak.

Crisp leaves flutter, dance with glee,
Mischief hides among the greenery.
Sip it slow, it's quite the tease,
Refreshing laughter in the breeze.

The Elixir of Sunny Days

Bubbles tickle as we sip,
Taste of summer on our lip.
Round delight in colorful bowls,
As we escape from everyday roles.

Golden rays and laughter blend,
Every drop a playful mend.
Crisp and cool, a joyous spree,
Bringing smiles, oh can't you see?

Vibrant Breezes at Dusk

Sunset glows in shades of fun,
Breezes twirl as day is done.
The cool refreshment sings so bright,
Laughter dances into the night.

A skewer stacked with joyful bites,
Tasting summer's silly delights.
With each laugh, the stars we chase,
In twilight's glow, we find our grace.

Garden's Bounty in a Splash

In the patch where colors pop,
Round green orbs laugh, never stop.
Splashing joy in the sun's warm glow,
Tickled tongues taste summer's show.

Juicy joy with a crunchy bite,
Happiness grows with every delight.
The garden's laughter fills the air,
A playful feast beyond compare.

Cool Caress of Nature's Hand

Nature's fingers wave so bright,
Tapping rhythm of pure delight.
Leaves sway gently, a teasing dance,
Creating smiles, a merry chance.

Liquid freedom drips and rolls,
A ticklish tease for thirsty souls.
Under the sun's watchful glance,
Joyful pops hold a silly stance.

Fragrant Summer's Kiss

Scented breezes playfully greet,
Fragrance whispers, oh so sweet.
Giggling greens in the warm sun,
Flavor burst is pure, simple fun.

Juicy bites and laughter blend,
Tasty quirks, a playful trend.
Sweetness tickles, laughter spills,
Nature's humor gives us thrills.

Sunlit Delight and Refreshment

Bright sunbeans dance on shiny skin,
While playful critters join in the spin.
Giggles rise with every taste,
In this slice of zest, none go to waste.

Coolness bursts with each juicy drip,
That's the secret of summer's trip.
Happy munches, a tasty spree,
Laughter and joy, wild and free.

Fragrant Slices of Joy

In the garden, a striped delight,
Giggles rise with each juicy bite.
Round and sweet, they dance in air,
Throwing smiles without a care.

A picnic spread, so bold and bright,
Sticky fingers, oh what a sight!
Laughter echoes, birds take flight,
Nature's candy, pure delight!

Nectarine Dreams

Sunkissed orbs with a wink in tow,
Dripping sweetness, oh what a show!
Chasing taste, like kids at play,
Dreaming up games, it's our way!

Funny faces, a comical scene,
Squirting juice like a quirky machine!
Rolling laughter, a juicy spree,
Life's a circus, come join me!

The Cool Green Bliss

Chilled concoctions in frosty glass,
Giggling friends as we raise a sass.
Slurping loud, it's a fun parade,
Witty banter, the jokes are made!

Chilling out in the summer heat,
Funny hats and dancing feet.
Every sip, a joyous cheer,
With each gulp, we invite the weird!

Oasis in the Sun

A quirky slice on a vibrant plate,
Sunshine smiles, oh, what a fate!
Silly hats, we twirl around,
Sipping joy with laughter abound.

Splashes of colors bright and wild,
Nonsense jokes, like a playful child.
In this oasis, fun's the theme,
Life's a giggle, a playful dream!

Lush Harmony of Chill and Cheer

In a garden where giggles bloom,
There's a fruit with a goofy plume.
It rolls and wobbles, oh what a sight,
Bringing smiles from morning to night.

A twist of leaves with a splash of glee,
Dances in the breeze like it's one with the bee.
It tickles your tongue, makes you grin,
A summer party, let the fun begin!

Nature's Gift in Juicy Hues

A round, jolly orb so bright,
With a laughter that takes flight.
Juicy drops fall like rain,
Silly faces, no room for pain.

It hides in patches, so sweet and bold,
Whispers secrets that never get old.
With each saucy bite, the joy unfurls,
A fruity fiesta for all the worlds.

Crisp Shadows Under the Sun

Beneath the sun, a playful chase,
Fruit bounces around, in a silly space.
Its green cap whirls in the summer air,
Sprinkling joy with a funky flair.

In shady spots where laughter thrives,
You'll find this gem with rambunctious vibes.
Gather round for a juicy treat,
With a giggle and munch, life feels complete!

The Savor of Hidden Meadows

In meadows bright where giggles blend,
Lives a flavor that's hard to comprehend.
It's green and jolly, oh what a twist,
One taste and you get hooked, none can resist!

With every bite, a dance begins,
A fruity chuckle, the fun just spins.
So take a scoop, let your tongue play,
In this hidden world, we'll laugh all day!

Soothing Orchard Breeze

In a garden where the sun does play,
Frogs in shades of green sing all day.
A fruit so sweet, it rolls down the lane,
While bees dance around, buzzing in vain.

The leaves tickle the air with a gentle tease,
And squirrels debate, 'Is it really cheese?'
Laughter echoes through the boughs so wide,
As butterflies wear coats of joy with pride.

The breeze whispers secrets of fruit-filled dreams,
While crickets recite their comedic themes.
A splash of green joy splattered near the ground,
In this whimsical world, pure silliness is found.

A Symphony of Green

A plump little orb with a cheeky grin,
Happily rolls as the fun begins.
In the symphony of laughter beneath the trees,
Caterpillars waltz with charming ease.

The mockingbird cackles, a quirky tune,
As shadows dance beneath the bright, round moon.
Cucumbers giggle, pickles join along,
In this green dance, nothing feels wrong.

A patch of silliness, nature's delight,
Where every critter has its bit of light.
Chasing shadows, the fruit takes a dive,
Spreading the joy that teaches us to thrive.

Lush Escape

In a secret spot where the wild things grow,
Laughter sprouts up, putting on a show.
A jolly fruit bursts out with a flair,
While critters giggle, without any care.

The zephyr tickles as it sweeps through,
Whispers of chaos in emerald hue.
A frog in a crown takes the stage with glee,
While ants tap dance to the rhythm of three.

A land of whimsy where all is bizarre,
Each leaf a stage, each flower a star.
In this vibrant place, coconuts jest,
Nature's comedy put to the test.

Essence of Twilight

As twilight descends on a fruity parade,
Underneath stars, the laughter is laid.
A wobbly ball joins the dance of the night,
With fireflies buzzing, a comical sight.

A twist of green curls in the cool air,
Bouncing along without a single care.
The world is a stage, the silliness reigns,
Where giggles break out like unexpected trains.

This nighttime realm is a vibrant affair,
Where minty whispers tease without a care.
With every chuckle, a bright star ignites,
In this patch of cheer, everything delights.

Verdant Echoes

In a patch of green where joy is found,
Laughter grows up from the ground.
With leaves that tickle and fruits that tease,
Nature's giggle in the gentle breeze.

Juggling flavors, a dance so bold,
Chasing sunshine, not caring for cold.
A splash of sweetness, a dash of flair,
Playful party, with zest in the air.

Sizzling Warmth

Under the sun, where the crazies play,
Round and juicy, they brighten the day.
Giggling globes of vibrant glee,
Wobble and wiggle, oh so carefree.

A slice of laughter, a bite of cheer,
Juicy chaos, oh bring it near!
Rolling around like clowns on the floor,
In this fruity riot, who could ask for more?

Cool Comfort

Chilling in shade, with friends all around,
Juicy bursts burst without making a sound.
Blushing and bouncing, a laughter parade,
Sips of delight, in the summer charade.

Dancing droplets, with giggles they cling,
Wobbling treats make the heart want to sing.
A splash of refreshment, a smile so bright,
Under the moon, we're longing for night.

The Lush Elixir

In a glass of joy, a swirl and a spin,
Fizzy delight that tickles the chin.
A riot of colors, a burst of laughs,
With every sip, the silly heart quaffs.

Bubbling spirits, dancing with cheer,
Frothy concoctions, come sip them here!
Totally zany, a jester's parade,
With a wink and a smile, let fun never fade!

Fragrance of the Earth

Whiffs of laughter in the warm sun's glow,
Where crazy breezes decide to flow.
Silly scents prance, playful and free,
Round and round, they giggle with glee.

The earth's own candy, colors explode,
Rolling in clovers, they lighten the load.
Every whiff's a wink as they float on the air,
Nature's funny jokes keep us in the fair!

The Green Caress

In a garden where giggles grow,
A dance with leaves, a minty show.
Laughter swirls like the summer breeze,
Tickling toes with such joyful ease.

Fruits in a bowl, they play and tease,
With juicy antics, they aim to please.
One rolls away, oh what a sight!
Chasing it down, a comical flight.

Glimmers of green in the midday sun,
Sipping on joy, oh what a fun!
Each crunch comes with a silly sound,
Who knew such laughter could be found?

So let us feast, let's shout hooray,
For playful greens in bright array.
Life is better with giggles and cheer,
In this zesty world, we have no fear.

Worlds of Flavor

In a land where flavors dance and sing,
Everything's merry, from winter to spring.
Bouncing berries and a citrus grin,
Together they form a taste-spinning spin.

A splash of zest in a sunny bowl,
A wobbly taste that tickles the soul.
Crunch on the green, oh such delight,
Mix, shake, and whirl, what a silly sight!

Summertime promises a frothy delight,
Sipping concoctions all day and night.
In this realm of taste, let's take a dive,
Where the quirky fruits come alive and thrive.

Spoon in hand, we're explorers brave,
Navigating flavors like a tasty wave.
Giggles erupt with each silly bite,
In this world of flavor, everything's right!

Morning's Dewy Romance

Dew drops wink like mischievous eyes,
As they sparkle in the morning skies.
A cheeky fruit blushes, so sweet and bright,
Calling all critters for morning's light.

Laughter erupts, as the sun peeks through,
With a splash of juice, what fun to chew!
Blend, whip, and twirl, in a happy chance,
Every scoop leads to a silly dance.

Each bite brings giggles, sweet and clear,
The morning air fills with festive cheer.
Savor the flavor of bright dewy scenes,
In this playful game, we harvest our dreams.

A toast to the day, in colorful stew,
Where romance is found in each vibrant hue.
So raise your cups to the silly and sweet,
In the morning's embrace, life's a tasty treat!

Whirlwind of Green

In a storm of green, the flavors collide,
Kooky concoctions that cannot hide.
Witness the twist as they jive and sway,
Mixing and mingling in a fanciful way.

Laughing leaves in a jug so round,
Bright and nutty, what joy we found.
Bouncing with glee, they burst into song,
In this wacky kitchen, we all belong.

A pinch of chaos, a dash of fun,
An explosion of taste before we've begun.
Slide on the surface of laughter and zest,
In a whirlwind of whimsy, we're truly blessed.

So let's spin our spoons and shout with glee,
For a wacky world where we're all fruity.
In the cyclone of flavors, we lift our cheer,
For the madness of greens brings us all near.

Lively Succulence

A juicy bite, a fruity spree,
Dancing flavors, wild and free.
Green delight in every chew,
Laughter bursts, as friends ensue.

Squishy plumps in every scoop,
Dripping sweetness, what a loop!
Giggling bites, more hugs around,
This zesty treat is joy unbound.

Silly faces as we munch,
Who knew fruit could pack a punch?
With every slice, our grins expand,
It's a party, oh so grand!

A slippery race, we giggle and chase,
Juice flying high, oh what a mess!
Sticky fingers, laughter loud,
Who can resist this giggly crowd?

Vivid Flavor Escapade

Bright and bold on picnic day,
Cheery bites, come join the play!
Textures twist in flavor cheer,
Catch a slice, and give a cheer!

A burst of joy, a sweet rampage,
Tickled taste buds, such a stage!
Gobbling down with silly grins,
This juicy fun always wins.

As we tumble in fruity bliss,
Surprises found in every kiss,
Green and juicy, silly delight,
Chasing laughter, what a sight!

With fruit in hand, we dance about,
Trading slices, never doubt,
What a taste, what a thrill,
In every bite, a joyous spill!

Glistening Sunshine

Golden orbs, a sunny tease,
Splash of laughter, purest breeze.
Juicy dribbles and goofy grins,
Sunshine wrapped in fruity skins.

We take a bite, the world's a stage,
Silly faces set the gauge!
Roll and tumble, in a fruit fight,
With every chunk, our hearts feel light!

A splash of joy, a sip of glee,
Pranks unfold, spontaneous spree.
Juicy joy, our spirits soar,
We can't settle for just one more!

In every slice, a bright embrace,
Slippery giggles weave and race.
Adventures hold this cheerful flair,
Under the sun, without a care!

Nature's Palette of Flavor

In a garden where laughter blooms,
Flavors dance in sunny rooms.
Nature's brush paints burst and zest,
Silly bites, we've found the best!

A carousel of juicy glee,
Tasting fun, so wild and free!
Green and splashy, chuckles rise,
Every nibble is a surprise!

Belly laughs with every piece,
Sharing joy, a sweet release.
Wobbling bites, a sticky spree,
Savoring humor with fruity glee!

Chasing bites that slip and slide,
Full of laughter, we cannot hide.
Nature's glee in every taste,
Wraps us up in endless haste!

Refreshing Hues of Summer's Palette

In a bowl of laughter, colors collide,
A cheeky slice of joy, oh what a ride!
Green giggles dance on the tongue so bright,
Fruit and leaves frolic in the warm sunlight.

Splashing into summer's vibrant delight,
A twist here, a squeeze there, oh what a sight!
Juicy secrets hidden in every bite,
Nature's confetti, a taste that feels right.

Summer's Lush Embrace

Beneath the sun's warm, mischievous gaze,
Leaves play hide and seek in leafy maze.
With a wink and a wiggle, they dare to share,
Chilled whispers of sweetness fill the air.

Drunken bees buzzing, in floral ballet,
As veggies and fruits laugh the day away.
Silly sips of bliss on a sun-drenched spree,
Refreshing concoctions, oh, come join me!

Green Garden Whispers

In the garden of giggles, secrets abound,
Where the green friends chuckle without a sound.
They plot their mischief beneath the bright sky,
With a pop and a squirt, oh me, oh my!

Bursts of surprise with each tasty bite,
A splash of silliness - what pure delight!
Nature's pranksters, in a fruity parade,
Wait for no one, let the fun cascade!

Chill of the Harvest

When the harvest is ripe, the laughter's loud,
In the crates of cheer, we gather our crowd.
With frosty treats that dance in the sun,
A wink from the fridge, oh what fun is begun!

A blend of giggles swirls in the mix,
With pops and crackles, it's all in the fix.
Refreshing delights, oh, they whirl and sway,
Let's toast to the antics of this summer's day!

Whispering Breezes Amidst the Orchard

In a garden where laughter grows,
Twirling fruits in a playful pose.
Leaves whisper jokes to the sunlit air,
While bees dance round like they haven't a care.

A bushy twist and a fruity swirl,
Nature's giggle is a colorful whirl.
The zany flavors duke it out,
In this fruity fest, there's no room for doubt.

A frolicsome breeze pulls me along,
To a world where everything feels so wrong.
Bite into joy, let your taste buds sing,
Here in the orchard, it's a silly fling.

Juicy bites and a ticklish kiss,
Who needs perfection when you've got this?
Every crunch tickles, every drip's a thrill,
Laughter and flavor, there's plenty to spill.

Cool Delights from the Earth

Underneath the blazing sun,
Beneath the green, where the fun is spun.
Crunchy treats and wobbly cheer,
Earth's own magic, perfectly clear.

Laughter bubbles in every bite,
A splash of zest, oh what a sight!
Nature's jester dressed in green,
Giggling sweetness, a quirky scene.

While sipping breezes with a grin,
The fun begins from deep within.
From the earth, we craft our feast,
For silly jokes and joy, at least!

With every munch, the giggles rise,
Sprinkling joy with a splash of surprise.
In this quirky patch, we all unite,
To savor the odd and delightfully light.

Sips of Verdant Paradise

A flavor twist that makes you smile,
Tasty wonders that last a while.
In the garden, fun seems to bloom,
Sip it up, let's dispel the gloom.

Green concoctions in a cheeky glass,
In this haven, everyone will pass.
Chuckle with friends, raise a toast,
To the goofy flavors that we love most.

Laughter bubbles, we take a sip,
Funny stories on every lip.
Nature's bounty, a slippery ride,
With giggles shared, let joy abide.

Every gulp's a whimsical chase,
Dancing flavors in a slick embrace.
In paradise, we savor each jest,
A refreshing bite, we feel so blessed.

Nature's Chill in Every Bite

When summer days get too absurd,
Take a break, let's taste the word.
A twist of glee in every nibble,
Tickling tongues with a cheerful dribble.

Outside the box, the flavors play,
In this haven, let's be silly all day.
With every crunch, a laugh resounds,
In nature's chill, pure joy abounds.

A playful chase on a breezy spree,
Jemmy, jammy wonders await you and me.
Silly sweetness, a cocktail surprise,
With every mouthful, joy multiplies.

Come share the fun, make it a treat,
With nature's humor, life's so sweet.
In each bite, a joke unfolds,
A tantalizing tale that never gets old.

Scented Joys

In a garden of laughter, green and bright,
Grow fruits with a grin, a wondrous sight.
They giggle and wiggle, under sun's warm play,
Juicy bursts of joy, in a playful array.

A zesty breeze dances, full of cheer,
Whispers tales of flavor, so sincere.
With every rosy slice, a laugh is shared,
A fruity delight, with giggles ensnared.

In bowls of delight, a sprinkle of fun,
They tease every tongue, oh what a run!
Each bite brings a chuckle, so sweet, so light,
Creating a festival, from morning till night.

So let's toast to the bliss, so vivid and bold,
With flavors that shimmer, like stories retold.
In this fragrant delight, let your spirit soar,
With every joyful bite, you'll always want more.

A Splash of Verdure

In a bowl of green giggles, life takes a dive,
Crunchy and silly, they come alive.
Chilled and delighted, each piece a treat,
Dancing on tongues with a jumpy beat.

Sprinkle some sparkle, a dash of surprise,
With juicy confetti, right before your eyes.
Every slice a moment, a splash to savor,
Creating a symphony, a giggly flavor.

Bouncing and blending, what a crazy mix,
A carnival of tastes, a whimsical fix.
Each munch sends you soaring, on clouds above,
United in laughter, and flavors we love.

So gather the friends, in the sun's bright glow,
Share slices of laughter, let the joy overflow.
In this puzzle of flavors, let fun be your guide,
With every cheerful bite, let happiness glide.

Harmony in Every Bite

In a chorus of crunch, the laughter will ring,
With green little gems, that jump and sing.
A symphony formed, in bowls that delight,
Each mouthful a tune, sweetening the night.

Tangy and bright, they tango with cheer,
A perfect duet, you'll want to hear.
Bite after bite, a harmony grows,
With every sweet nibble, the laughter flows.

In picnics of joy, the giggles collide,
Twirling with friends, where silliness hides.
A party of flavors, that tickle the tongue,
In this colorful mix, we'll forever be young.

So let's share a toast, to this fruity parade,
With smiles and laughter, together we're made.
In each splendid chunk, fun finds its way,
In every sweet morsel, a colorful play.

Liquid Jewel of the Season

In a pitcher of laughter, colors collide,
With splashes of giggles, side by side.
Each sip a twist, a playful delight,
Creating a buzz, in the sunny light.

Bubbles of joy, dance in the sun,
Refreshing the soul, oh what fun!
With every cool droplet, the smiles unfold,
In a tapestry woven, with stories untold.

As the fun flows freely, let worries drift,
Through sips of enchantment, feel the uplift.
A toast to the moments, that sparkle and shine,
In this liquid treasure, let our hearts align.

So fill up your glass, let the joy ignite,
With cheers of delight, and bubbles so bright.
In each playful swirl, a magic unfurls,
In this jewel of the season, let laughter twirls.

Garden's Breath of Freshness

In a patch of color bright,
Laughter dances, sheer delight.
A splash of green, a grin so wide,
Nature's treats, we can't abide.

With every crunch, a giggle grows,
Unexpected flavors in the throes.
A secret recipe from the ground,
In every bite, joy can be found.

The garden hums a silly tune,
As bees and bugs all dance and croon.
Frolic in this tasty space,
Where smiles are served with every grace.

So gather round, let's have some fun,
Underneath the shining sun.
A feast of laughter, light, and zest,
In this patch of life, we feel our best.

Juicy Serenade

A splash of color on a plate,
Like sunshine's kiss, it's quite the fate.
Sweet and sassy, bold and bright,
Every bite brings pure delight.

With flavors swirling, what a show!
It's like a party, don't you know?
Unexpected bursts, oh what a treat,
A juicy dance that can't be beat.

Chomping, munching, giggling loud,
This fruity symphony makes us proud.
Laughter echoes, filling the air,
In each sweet bite, joy everywhere.

So let's engage in this light buffet,
Where fun and flavor come to play.
With every mouthful, life's a song,
In this tasty world, we all belong.

The Taste of Sunlit Days

Beneath the sun, a vibrant feast,\nA quirky crunch, to say the least.
Brighten up the dullest mood,
With each sweet nibble, we're renewed.

The laughter flows, it's quite the scene,
With winks and giggles in between.
A twist of flavor, what a game,
In every crisp, we stake our claim.

Juicy treasures in the sun,
Playing tug-of-war, it's so much fun.
Whimsical bites that burst and shine,
Silly moments are truly divine.

So gather friends, let's share the cheer,
With every taste, we hold so dear.
A juicy world that brings us praise,
In every nibble, sunlit days.

Sweetness in the Shade

In leafy hideouts, delicious treats,
Beneath cool branches where laughter greets.
A secret stash, a hidden joy,
Nature's goodness, for every girl and boy.

Whimsical flavors, bright and fun,
Tickling noses, one by one.
Sweet and zesty laughs abound,
In this shady nook, joy is found.

The sun may blaze, but here it's chill,
A fruity delight that fits the bill.
Each bite a giggle, each taste a cheer,
In every mouthful, joy draws near.

So come and join this playful quest,
In this shaded realm, be our guest.
With laughter and sweetness all around,
In every morsel, happiness is found.

A Symphony of Green and Gold

In a garden, things collide,
A fruit so round, it can't hide.
Twirling vines in a playful dance,
Tickling noses – what a chance!

A juicy splash, oh what a scene,
Nature's charm, so bright and green.
With laughter loud, the sun smiles wide,
As giggles bounce, they won't subside.

Slicing joy, it spills and rolls,
Refreshing sweetness fills our bowls.
Green leaves prance, oh, join the fun,
A quirky feast for everyone!

So let's toast with sips so bright,
A fragrant picnic, pure delight.
Come gather 'round, it's time to play,
In this silly, fruity cabaret!

Summer's Glistening Essence

A bowl of sunshine, round and sweet,
Citrus joys with a minty beat.
Plump and ready, they can't be tamed,
With giggles sprouting, they're unclaimed!

Sweaty brows and laughter wide,
Chasing flavors, come enjoy the ride.
A splash of zest, a dash of cheer,
With every bite, the fun draws near!

Popsicles drip with a sticky grace,
While sticky fingers race to chase.
Sticky joys that leave their mark,
In this playful kitchen-park!

So let's summon summer's glee,
In every crunch, a melody.
An anthem sung in bright daylight,
As laughter dances, pure delight!

Fragrant Notes of Warm Sun

Oh, what a fragrant sun-kissed treat,
A jolly bite that's hard to beat!
Mixing flavors, a quirky show,
With giggles that simply overflow.

Nature's candy, fresh and light,
In cups and bowls, such a sight!
With zany shapes, it brings a grin,
Eager hearts let the fun begin!

Sunnies sipping on sweet brews,
While twirling round in colorful hues.
Whispers of playful scents abound,
In this jolly feast, joy is found!

So gather close, let laughter soar,
In green and gold, forevermore.
With winks of whimsy, we will sing,
Of summer cheer that joy can bring!

Sweet Relief in a Bowl

Round and plump, a splash in sight,
Bouncing flavors, pure delight.
Chilled and ready, the crowd arrives,
With happy hearts, the feast survives!

Laughter bubbles, oh what a show,
As juicy bits begin to flow.
Minty whispers swirl and tease,
Tickling taste buds with such ease!

Refreshing sips, a twist of glee,
While munching bites, wild and free.
Adventurous snacks, vibrant and bold,
Making memories that never grow old!

So grab your spoon, invite a friend,
In this fun bowl, the joy won't end.
With every scoop, let laughter ring,
In our hearts, the summer's king!

Juicy Whispers of the Garden

In the garden where sweetness plays,
Giggles burst in the sun's rays.
Fruity bites wiggle and dance,
Making each moment a silly chance.

Laughter rolls among the leaves,
As I feast on nature's heaves.
The juice runs down in joyful streams,
Imagining all the wacky dreams.

Bouncing bees in a cheeky hurry,
Making the blooms look rather blurry.
With every nom, a bright grin shows,
In the patch where the wild joy grows.

A squishy treat slips from my grip,
How can something be so hip?
The critters cheer for a juicy bite,
In this garden, it all feels right.

Refreshing Twilight Serenade

Under the twilight's playful glance,
Tasty giggles begin to dance.
With each slice, a chuckle bursts,
In the coolness, we quench our thirsts.

The bowl is filled with silly chunk,
Even the stars seem to get punk'd.
Oh, how the flavors swirl and spin,
As we start the silly din.

Laughter echoes with every bite,
Oh, this evening feels so right!
The moon beams down a playful wink,
As we munch and laugh and think.

Bright green pops, oh what a sight,
Tickling taste buds, pure delight.
In the fading light, we dig in deep,
Promises of laughter we'll always keep.

Cool Breeze and Sweet Slices

A cool breeze whispers through the trees,
As juicy slices bring me to my knees.
The little bits giggle, oh what a show,
Making mouths water with every flow.

Wacky critters join the bite,
Capering about in pure delight.
Each piece slinks away in disguise,
With silly faces and bright green ties.

Squirrels chuckle from the highest branch,
Witnessing this fruity, friendly dance.
With every crunch, a joke is spun,
A comedy night, all in good fun!

Chilly nibbles on sunny days,
Mirth is found in oh-so-many ways.
In every slice, a giggle hides,
As joy and laughter take wild rides.

Verdant Delight on the Tongue

In my bowl, a splash of cheer,
Bright bits smile from ear to ear.
Each juicy morsel sings with glee,
Turning my snack to a comedy spree.

Green goodness turns the frown upside down,
Jokes jump out in this tasty town.
With every playful pop and squish,
I make the silliest of every wish.

The crunch echoes, a joyous call,
Even the shy ones begin to sprawl.
With giggles abundant and laughter afloat,
A garden party, my favorite note!

The taste of sunshine on my tongue,
Oh, these tales of sweet bites sung.
With every nibble, a joy so bright,
The fun continues into the night.

Cool Bliss on the Palate

In the heat of the day, a bright round treat,
With a splash of green, it can't be beat.
Juicy bites dance, oh what a delight,
Laughing and munching, everything feels right.

A splash of coolness, a giggle ensues,
Toss in some laughter and happy peruse.
Sweetness that tickles, a burst on my tongue,
In summer's embrace, forever I'm young.

Sprightly Summer's Gift

In sun-soaked gardens, a treasure unfolds,
Frolicking flavors, a story untold.
Green and round wonders with laughter reside,
Bouncing in bowls, our joy cannot hide.

Zesty surprises burst open with cheer,
Tickling taste buds, we all gather near.
Chillin' and thrillin', a banquet of glee,
Who knew that summer could feel so carefree?

Earthy Revelations

From humble beginnings, their tales intertwine,
Nature's own jester, how playful they shine.
Hidden in gardens, they party all night,
While we feast and chuckle, it all feels just right.

Each scoop brings a chuckle, a whimsical tale,
What joy in the crunch, a delectable trail.
Harvested giggles on each summer day,
With nature's confetti, we laugh all the way.

Radiant Refreshment

Bright orbs of joy, like a burst of the sun,
In every bright moment, our laughter's begun.
With a dash of the green, oh look at them dance,
Together they whirl, in a fruity romance.

Sipping on delights, as the giggles take flight,
A splash of the silly, it all feels so right.
In this joyous feast, we smile without end,
These vibrant companions, they always transcend.

Essence of Leisure

In a world where flavors dance and play,
A juicy orb winks in the sun's ray.
Crisp green whispers tickle your nose,
While laughter bursts as the cool breeze flows.

Slices grinning like a cheeky grin,
Quenching thirst with a cheeky spin.
Juice dribbles down your chin in delight,
Chasing worries away, oh what a sight!

Picnics scatter on plaid blankets wide,
Juicy bites and giggles collide.
Nature's candies wrapped in delight,
With coolness that makes everything right.

Sneaky summer snacks in a sack,
Who brought the goodies? I've lost track!
Laughter bubbles with each silly bite,
Essence of joy, oh what a night!

The Gleaming Garden

In a patch where colors cheerfully bloom,
Green sends giggles to chase away gloom.
Amidst the chaos, a shiny delight,
Roll it over; it giggles at night.

Breezy whispers tickle each leaf,
Grumpy bugs scowl in disbelief.
A secret potion, a splash of cheer,
Nature's prank; it's summer's sneer!

Tongues wagging as flavors collide,
In this garden, joy takes a ride.
Visions of laughter along the way,
Where sweetness dances and children play.

Allies in sunshine, oh what a treat,
When colors pop, life is complete.
The gleaming bounty, a feast of fun,
Happiness shines like a bright, warm sun!

A Breath of Refreshment

A zesty breeze takes center stage,
With a smile as bright as a sunlit page.
Lively aromas fill up the air,
Tickling the senses, beyond compare.

Sips of sparkle and laughter entwined,
A bubbly companion, refreshment defined.
Slurping joy from cups held high,
While dribbles and giggles float up to the sky.

Chasing droplets with playful intent,
Even the sun seems to be bent.
A chemistry made of sweetness and zest,
In this moment, we feel truly blessed.

So raise your glass, make a toast,
To drinks that we love and cherish the most!
In a swirl of joy, let nothing prevent,
A breath of refreshment, oh how it went!

Nature's Sweet Reward

Frolicking fruits on a sunny spree,
Cheeky bites, come share with me!
A slice of laughter on a delightful day,
Where sweetness blooms in a comical way.

Nature giggles in her lovely attire,
Gifts of joy that never tire.
In every nibble, a story unfolds,
With hints of mischief, daring and bold.

Gather around, the table is set,
Creamy delights that you won't forget.
As we feast on the funny and fine,
Nature's the host of a grand ol' time.

So join in the fun, toss cares to the breeze,
Pleasures abound; oh, don't you agree?
In every bite, a giggle—or two,
Nature's sweet reward, shared by me and you.

Refreshing Summer Ambrosia

A green delight on sunny days,
Tickling taste buds in wild ways.
Juicy bites and laughter flow,
Sweet and cool, a vibrant show.

What a combo, oh what a feast,
A sunny picnic, to say the least!
Chuckle as you dribble and spill,
It's messy fun—oh what a thrill!

Toss some seeds, make a little game,
Silly faces, who's to blame?
Juicy juice all over the place,
Laughter echoes, oh, such grace!

At the end, we all agree,
This goofy treat is the key.
So grab a slice, come join the cheer,
Our silly summer vibes are here!

Slices of Serenity

In the shade, a slice awaits,
As laughter dances, teasing fates.
Beneath bright sun, we take a bite,
Each juicy squirt, pure delight!

With laughs erupting, seeds do fly,
Who knew fruit could make you cry?
Wipe your chin, let's take a stand,
A fruity face-off—what a plan!

We juggle slices, oh what fun,
Accidental toss—oh, there it runs!
Squishy quirks, don't take offense,
In fruity battles, we find suspense!

Endless giggles fill the air,
Sticky fingers everywhere!
As the sun sets, we'll reminisce,
About each juicy, silly bliss!

Crisp Harmony in the Heat

Under the sun, a crunch awaits,
Sassy slices, no debates.
With a zing, they steal the show,
Who knew laughter could overflow?

Green and juicy, bright and bold,
A comedy in every fold.
Salty breezes, silly tunes,
We dance around like goofball loons!

An accidental toss, oops! Don't fret,
The funniest moment we won't forget!
Laughter echoes through the park,
While sticky fingers leave their mark.

As the sun dips, the laughter thrives,
This sweet madness is how we survive.
With each slice, our spirits soar,
In this crisp world, who could ask for more?

Verdant Reflections

Staring at the green and sweet,
Splashes of joy in each bite meet.
With each chuckle, the juices spray,
Who knew happiness could betray?

The sun's a-joke, the breeze does laugh,
As we garnish our silly path.
Each hefty slice, a perfect score,
The green team's antics we adore!

With giggles cascading all around,
The mess we make, a sight profound.
Sticky glories on our face,
In our fruity world, there's no disgrace!

At summer's end, we'll share the tales,
Of fruity feasts and laughter trails.
So here's to joy, in every bite,
A verdant play under the light!

Whispering Groves

In a grove where laughter grows,
Fruits frolic with the breeze,
One wore stripes and one wore spots,
Swaying like they've got some keys.

A jolly chef with a big hat,
Sliced them up with endless glee,
Said, "What's better? A winter hat,
Or a cool slice by the sea?"

They danced around the picnic spread,
In a juicy, cheeky spree,
Bouncing high while others fled,
Making juice, so wild and free.

At sunset, giggles filled the air,
As they served up flavors bright,
A party no one could compare,
In the grove of pure delight!

The Taste of Morning

In the morning sun's embrace,
A liquid splash, a sweet surprise,
A splash of green with hints of grace,
Makes sleepy heads begin to rise.

Cup in hand, they take a sip,
"What a mix! My taste buds cheer!"
The flavor does a joyful flip,
As morning giggles fill the sphere.

Tangled straws, a twisty mess,
They're laughing till they can't no more,
Too much zest? A fun distress,
Many trips to the fridge door.

Three cheers for tastes that stay so fresh,
A morning drink of pure delight,
With every drop, a giggle's flesh,
Chasing away the sleepy night!

Nature's Zestful Fusion

In the garden, colors flash,
Leaves do shimmy, fruits collide,
A mishmash party, what a splash,
A green and orange joyride.

They tossed a seed and watched it spin,
Bouncing high, oh what a sight!
Together they laughed, a fruity grin,
Twirling through the day and night.

Every drop's a funny tale,
With bubbles popping everywhere,
Nature's dance will never fail,
Each sip brings another dare.

Come join the feast of silly sights,
Where flavors blend with playful cheer,
A fusion full of pure delights,
In this garden, life is clear!

Vital Liquid Harvest

Gather 'round for the great parade,
Of green and orange, such a treat,
In glasses tall, they masquerade,
Hiding giggles beneath their sweet.

A summer splash, a wild chase,
Friends compete with splashing schemes,
Refreshing chaos sets the pace,
Each drop holds awoken dreams.

Straws that wiggle, slip and slide,
While everyone takes a big sip,
Laughter rings on every side,
As fruity fables start to grip.

When all is drank and time is gone,
They raise a toast to days that bloom,
With smiles that stretch from dusk till dawn,
In this harvest, there's always room!

The Cool Green Secret

In a patch where laughter grows,
A fruit that giggles, I suppose.
With laughter bursting at the seam,
It rolls and bounces like a dream.

Leaves that shimmy in a dance,
Spinning round as if in trance.
A secret recipe of cheer,
This playful treat brings all near.

Juicy chunks with a zesty twist,
Each bite a giggle, can't resist.
In summer's sun, we take a bite,
While critters join in sheer delight.

So grab a slice, come share a smile,
With every munch, we stay awhile.
Let laughter burst and shadows flee,
In this cool green jubilee.

Harvest of Delight

Round and bright, a jester's ball,
Rolling over, having a ball.
Beneath the sun, they laugh and play,
Squeezing joy in every way.

Gathered in the farmer's cart,
With silly faces, they impart.
A carnival of colors bright,
Each juicy slice, pure delight.

Chop and toss, the bowl's a scene,
A splash of giggles, vibrant green.
Friends and family gather 'round,
As laughter echoes through the ground.

Breezy days, we toss them high,
Clouds of joy float up to the sky.
In every bite, the fun ignites,
A harvest full of funny sights.

Whispering Fields

In fields where whispers dance in air,
A playful harvest, soft and rare.
Each fruit wears a grin so wide,
As breezes tease, and laughter rides.

Shadows stretch beneath the sun,
Rolling jokes, it's all in fun.
Nature's giggle fills the space,
A joy that nothing can erase.

With every crunch, a chuckle slips,
Juices dripping from our lips.
Neighbors join with hearty cheer,
In the hunt for joy, we steer.

The hidden gems beneath the leaves,
Share laughs and joy, everyone believes.
In whispering fields of cheer we thrive,
With each sweet slice, we come alive.

Garden's Embrace

In a garden where the giggles sprout,
Fruitful wonders, no doubt about.
With every turn, a punchline grows,
In nature's arms, the laughter flows.

Petals giggle, colors twist,
A flavor party, none can resist.
Chase the sun, let shadows play,
Moments brightening every day.

Green delights in tangled vines,
Swirling joys in fruity designs.
Hearts in bloom, the fun is grand,
A jovial dance, a merry band.

As dusk descends with cheeky grace,
In garden's arms, we find our place.
A nightly feast with jokes to share,
Wrapped in warmth, without a care.

Drenched in Dew

In the garden where giggles bloom,
Dewdrops dance like sprites in June.
A splash of green, a hint of sweet,
Nature's candy, oh what a treat!

With every bite, a chuckle spills,
Juicy laughter on the hills.
Round and ripe, they bounce around,
In this fruity circus, joy is found!

The squirrels join in, they want a share,
Juggling snacks without a care.
A picnic party full of cheer,
With every nibble, smiles appear!

As laughter echoes, the sun beams bright,
With each juicy bite, a playful bite.
In this garden of giggles and play,
Drenched in dew, we'll dance all day!

The Coolness of a Gentle Hand

A gentle breeze invites a grin,
Whispers of fun from where we begin.
Like icy treats on a summer's day,
Frolicsome flavors come out to play!

In the shade where the shadows twirl,
Chill delights in a leafy whirl.
Palms reaching out for a tangy hug,
Taste the coolness, feel the shrug!

Sipping sunshine with every bite,
A comedic twist in the daylight.
With every laugh, a splash we make,
A giggling slurp, for fun's own sake!

So here we gather on this fine day,
With a coolness that never fades away.
A gentle hand offers a sweet treat,
In this merry dance, we all feel fleet!

Green Delight Unveiled

Behind the leaves, a surprise so bright,
An emerald treasure with pure delight.
Underneath, the laughter hides,
With every bite, joy rides the tides!

Pick one up, let the fun commence,
A chuckle bubbles, it's pure suspense.
Green spheres rolling down the path,
Each one bursting with silly math!

Juggling flavors, a sweet regime,
Creating messes, the ultimate scheme.
Face full of joy, what a silly sight,
In laughter's grip, we twirl and write!

So gather 'round for the funny feast,
With smiles and giggles, we'll never cease.
Green delights that spin and prance,
In this whimsical, quirky dance!

Liquid Sunshine

From the pitcher, a splash of cheer,
Golden rays that draw you near.
Refreshing laughter pours with ease,
A tickle here, a giggle please!

Sip the warmth, feel the delight,
As flavors swirl, it's pure delight.
In every drop, a joyful quirk,
Where sunshine giggles and shadows lurk!

Serve it up with a wink and grin,
Liquid giggles, let the fun begin!
In every glass, a story flows,
Of summer days and playful prose!

So raise a toast to the sunny cheer,
Where laughter flows and friends draw near.
In this vibrant mix, the world feels fine,
Cheers to the joy in liquid sunshine!

Verdant Journeys

In a garden where flavors collide,
Juicy slices take us for a ride.
With a twist of green, oh what a delight,
Taste buds dancing in pure sunlight.

Giggles bubble like fizzy drinks,
Wobbling bowls and fruit-filled jinks.
A feast of laughter, a dash of cheer,
Every crunch says, 'Summer is here!'

Beneath the sun, we munch and share,
The sweetest secrets float in the air.
Silly faces with juice on the chin,
In this silly world, let the fun begin!

Running wild, we create a mess,
Sticky fingers? Oh, we must confess!
With every bite, the giggles grow,
Yummy chaos, here we go!

Soothing Summer Sweetness

A bowl of cheer, so cool and bright,
It makes dull days feel just right.
Beneath the shade, we laugh and play,
As silly squirrels steal our buffet.

Frolicsome friendships, a happy bunch,
Everyone's ready for a juicy munch.
Witty remarks as we take a bite,
Flavor explosions set hearts alight!

A chew, a crunch, and a giggly shout,
Sweetness covered in playful spout.
We play hopscotch on a flavor spree,
Chasing laughter as we dance with glee!

A sticky day, but who cares?
With fruit in hand, we conquer dares.
Grinning wide at the juicy score,
As summer waves, we beg for more!

Unveiling Crisp Tranquility

Breezy days with a flavor twist,
Chillin' snacks, you can't resist.
Fresh and silly, a playful tease,
Waves of laughter drift in the breeze.

Giggly moments in every bowl,
Crunching joys, that's our goal!
Sassy bites of crispy delight,
Snapping jokes from day to night.

With a splash of zing and a dash of fun,
Chasing shadows as we dash and run.
Jumpy, jolly, bursting with cheer,
Even bees buzz loud to draw near!

Oh, the sticky, sweet laughter we share,
As we weave tales of joy everywhere.
Nature's palette, a funny disguise,
In flavorful worlds, our spirits rise!

Serene Oasis

In a cozy nook where flavors bloom,
We gather 'round, chasing away gloom.
With giggles and bites, the fun won't end,
As our taste buds play, we blend and mend.

Crisp delights in our cheerful hands,
Summer flavors forming shiny bands.
Daring dalliances of flavor fun,
Under the sun, oh what a run!

With every slice, a chuckle unfolds,
Nature's stories, as each bite holds.
We spin and swirl, in playful delight,
Creating memories, joyous and bright.

So come take part in this lively feast,
Where joy's the star, and laughter's the beast.
In every crumb, the summer's jest,
An oasis of flavor, we are truly blessed!

Sweet Euphoria on the Palate

A slice so bright, a smile it brings,
Juicy surprise, like laughter sings.
Under the sun, a party starts,
Sweetness dances, and joy imparts.

With friends all around, we take a bite,
Chilling on ice, a summer's delight.
Green ribbons twirl, fresh and spry,
Tickling our taste buds, oh my, oh my!

Laughter erupts with each fruity cheer,
Droplets of juice, we give a leer.
Flavors collide in a tasty spin,
Eating with glee, let the fun begin!

What a combination, color parade,
Every bright bite, laughter is made.
The world's our stage, let's set the scene,
Sipping cool breezes, life's a cuisine!

Freshness Wrapped in Green

In the garden we roam, barefoot and free,
Life's little bursts as sweet as can be.
Leaves whisper secrets of flavors untold,
A symphony green that never gets old.

Munching delights, a crunch so loud,
Filling our hearts, we sing out proud.
Twirled in a salad, or straight on a plate,
The thrill of the fresh, let's celebrate fate!

Giggles erupt from bites of surprise,
Happiness found in each little prize.
Dancing with flavors, a colorful fight,
Oh what a feast, it feels just right!

As we cheer for the greens, we toast and we munch,
Funny, how joy comes in every crunch.
Keeping it light, and keeping it keen,
A riot of freshness, a glorious scene!

The Joy of Seasonal Abundance

In the market, colors leap and prance,
Nature's bounty, all in a dance.
The fruit of the land, so vibrant and grand,
Life's little nuggets, all at our hand.

Layers of joy in a bowl so wide,
A festival of tastes, come take a ride.
Swapping flavors like secrets in fun,
Bursting with laughter, laughter's begun!

Juggling the treats, we lift them high,
Sunny delights that catch the eye.
Bright and zesty, each mouthful a hit,
With every sweet nibble, we giggle and sit.

Cooking up fun, we gather around,
Creating a chaos, joy's newly found.
A buffet of seasons, our hearts they adorn,
Laughter and flavor, together reborn!

Oasis of Hidden Delight

Under the shade of a leafy expanse,
We find hidden treasures that make us dance.
Luscious and cool, the quirkiest treat,
Tickling our taste buds with every sweet beat.

Sipping on vibes and munching with glee,
Surprises abound in our jovial spree.
Tangled in laughter, we reach for the zest,
Joy in abundance, life's little quest.

Colors explode like fireworks bright,
Grabbing the moments, what a sight!
Taste buds rejoice in this playful fight,
Every small bite a reason to light.

So here's to the flavors, and here's to the fun,
With every sweet nibble, our hearts we've won.
A hidden oasis, a shimmering night,
Funny how joy comes in every bite!

www.ingramcontent.com/pod-product-compliance
Lightning Source LLC
Chambersburg PA
CBHW070005300426
43661CB00141B/235